Listening to Sound

by Karen A. Frenkel

Table of Contents

Introduction

What is sound? Have you ever wondered why some sounds are soft and others are loud? Why some sounds are deep and rich, and others are high and squeaky?

There are many different kinds of sounds and they make us feel certain ways. Sounds, like words, enable us to communicate. Music, for example, can communicate joy or sadness, even without words. When we find sounds annoying, we call them noise.

▲ When we talk, we use sound to communicate.

Read this book to learn about how sound acts. You will understand why we hear thunder after we see lightning. You will learn why there is silence.

You will also learn why different musical instruments make different sounds. You will understand what makes jet planes loud. We use sound in many ways. How many sounds can you hear right now? Listen and read on!

▲ Musical instruments have their own special sounds.

Chapter 1
What Is Sound?

Sound happens because of quick back-and-forth movements. These movements are called vibrations (vy-BRAY-shunz). They are a form of energy. Sound vibrations usually travel through air, but they also move through liquids and solids.

The vibrations occur in response to something else vibrating. When people clap their hands, for example, their hands vibrate. That makes the surrounding air vibrate, too. Applause fades when people stop clapping and the vibrations from their hands stop as well.

It's a Fact

Cats, dogs, and birds have vocal cords similar to ours. They purr, bark, and sing. Others animals create vibrations differently. Bees buzz by moving air with their wings. Whales "sing" by making moaning and chirping sounds, but we don't know exactly how.

Whales "sing" ▶
by sending
sound waves
through water.

When you speak, you force air from your lungs into your throat. The air passes through your **larynx** (LAIR-ingks), or voice box. Your larynx is the bump on your neck a few inches below your chin. You can feel your larynx vibrate when you push air through it in order to speak.

larynx

▲ You can feel your larynx vibrate as you speak.

No matter what they pass through, vibrations always travel in waves. As it travels, the vibrating front of a wave squeezes particles that are ahead. The particles become **compressed**. The compressed particles stay put for a moment and then spring apart. That movement affects neighboring particles, which are less compressed. Those particles are **rarefied** (RAIR-uh-fighd) compared to the compressed ones. The compression and rarefaction of particles cause the wave to move away from the source of the sound. As the wave weakens, the sound fades. The wave weakens because the vibrations have no more energy to push particles.

✔POINT

Reread
Reread the information about your larynx. Jot down some notes. Add to these notes as you read more about the larynx in Chapter 2. Then describe to a partner how your larynx works.

Experiment 1
Make a Telephone

- Get two paper cups.
- Punch a small hole through the bottom of each cup.
- Thread a long piece of string through the hole of one cup.
- Secure it with a knot.
- Do the same for the other cup.
- Now ask a friend to hold the cup to his ear.
- Hold the open end of your cup to your mouth and speak softly.
- Both of you should pull the string tight.

The vibrations of your voice travel along the string.

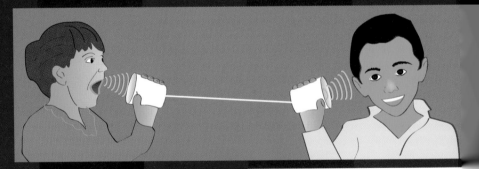

▲ Your friend hears the vibrations as your voice. You hear the vibrations as his voice. Telephones work the same way.

The Speed of Sound

The speed of sound depends on what it travels through. The more compressible something is, the slower the sound waves move. Particles of air are more compressible than particles of liquids. At room temperature, sound travels through air at 770 miles (1,239 kilometers) per hour. That is much slower than sound's speed through water, which is 3,315 miles (5,335 kilometers) per hour.

Sound travels faster through solids than through liquids. Sound moves through steel at 10,093 miles (16,243 kilometers) per hour. Even so, sound waves are much slower than light waves.

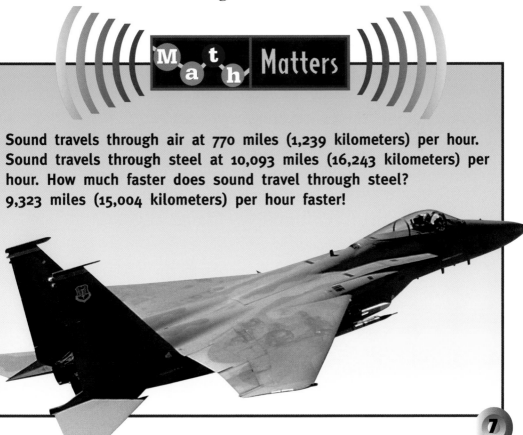

Math Matters

Sound travels through air at 770 miles (1,239 kilometers) per hour. Sound travels through steel at 10,093 miles (16,243 kilometers) per hour. How much faster does sound travel through steel? 9,323 miles (15,004 kilometers) per hour faster!

The only thing sound cannot travel through is outer space. **There is no air on the moon.** ▶ There is no air in space; therefore space is silent. It is called a **vacuum** (VA-kyoom). Without any particles to compress or rarefy, sound cannot travel. That's why astronauts speak to each other through special radios.

Sometimes there is a delay between an action and the sound it creates. Have you ever watched a baseball game and heard the crack of the bat just after it hit the ball? Perhaps you've seen lightning and heard thunder moments later. That's because light waves reach your eyes sooner than sound waves reach your ears. The thunderclap does not reach your ears instantly because sound takes longer than light to travel the same distance.

It's a Fact

We see lightning before we hear thunder because light travels faster than sound. Light travels through air at 186,000 miles (299,274 kilometers) per second. Sound travels through air at only 770 miles (1,239 kilometers) per hour.

Experiment 2
Reflecting Sound

Sound reflects off surfaces just like light reflects off mirrors.

- Take a long tube (from a roll of paper towels) or make a tube out of paper.
- Talk into one end of the tube. Does your voice sound louder or softer?
- Now place the tube over your ear.
- Walk over to the refrigerator or another appliance that hums. Does the hum seem louder or softer through the tube?
- Your voice and the appliance should sound louder. In both cases, the sound waves reflect against the sides of the tube. The sound waves at the end of the tube covering your ear are almost as strong as when they started.

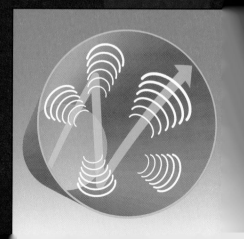

Echoes

We hear an echo when sound reflects, or bounces, off a hard surface. If you shout in a large, empty room, you hear your echo sooner than if you shout across a valley. It takes a while for sound to return if it reflects from far away. An echo is softer than your voice because not all the sound reflects. In a room, the walls absorb, or soak up, some sound waves. Across a valley, the trees, ground, and houses absorb some sound, too.

Ships and submarines transmit echoes through water. They use **sonar** (SOH-nar) to measure the depth of the ocean.

▲ Sonar can be used to locate schools of fish.

▲ Bats use echoes to avoid objects.

It's a Fact

Bats use echoes to help them fly and hunt food. When bats screech, the sound bounces off obstacles and insects. The bats track where things are based on how long the echoes take to return. That way the bats don't crash into things—and can find insects to eat.

Bending Sound Waves

When sound is absorbed, it **refracts** (rih-FRAKTS), or bends. Suppose you are in a room. When you speak, your voice travels more slowly through the air than through the walls. The direction that waves refract when they pass from one thing to another depends on whether they speed up or slow down.

Sound can also refract without moving through something else. Have you ever noticed that sounds seem louder at night? That's because different air temperatures refract sound differently.

▲ Your voice travels more slowly through the air than through walls.

Layers of air near the ground are cooler than the air higher up. When a sound wave rises, warmer air sends it back to the ground. The warm air bends the wave down. That's why it is easier to hear sounds over long distances at night, when the air is cooler.

Something similar happens in early mornings near water. Suppose you were standing on the shore of a lake at dawn. You might hear fishermen or other people on a boat speak, but you would not see them. That's because the cool water keeps the air near the water cool, too.

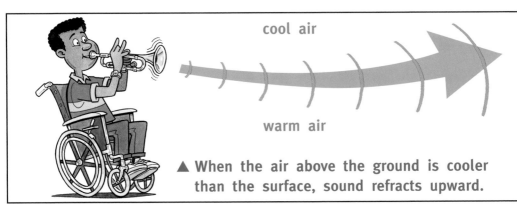

▲ When the air above the ground is cooler than the surface, sound refracts upward.

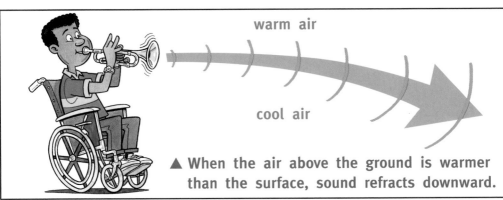

▲ When the air above the ground is warmer than the surface, sound refracts downward.

How Sound Waves Spread

You can hear sound around corners, too. When a sound wave hits the corner of a building, it curves around it. Think of the wave as reaching around the corner while it spreads wide. We call that **diffraction** (dih-FRAK-shun).

Sound passes through an opening the same way. The edges of an open door cause sound waves to diffract, too.

▲ Sound waves from this car diffract around the buildings. That's why, if you were standing around the corner on the avenue, you could hear the car approach.

Chapter 2
((((The Shapes))))
of Sound Waves

Sound waves in air act like waves in water. When you toss a pebble into a still pond, you see ripples spread out. The waves are circular, like a series of larger and larger rings. Sound waves also push away in curves from the source of a sound. The waves are spherical (SFEER-ih-kul), like a globe or bubble. They grow larger and larger. Scientists call such waves three-dimensional—that is, they push out in all directions. They spread up and down, sideways, and all around.

▼ Sound waves are shaped like bubbles, or spheres.

The highest part of a wave is the **crest**. The lowest part is the **trough** (TROFF). Particle compression and rarefaction happen at the crests and troughs.

Frequency

The distance from crest to crest or trough to trough is the **wavelength**. A wave with a short wavelength moves quickly from crest to crest or trough to trough. It passes a fixed point frequently, so we say it has a high **frequency**. A wave with a long wavelength moves from crest to crest or trough to trough less frequently, so it has a low frequency.

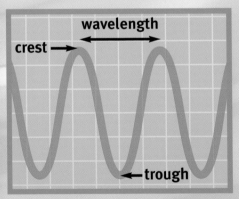

▲ Wavelength is the distance from crest to crest or trough to trough.

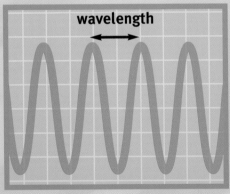

▲ This wave has twice the frequency of the wave on the left. It moves at a higher frequency. Its wavelength is half as long.

Pitch and Musical Notes

When something vibrates quickly, or with high frequency, a squeaky sound is produced. Slower vibrations produce low frequencies and deep sounds. Musicians say an instrument has a high or low **pitch**. Pitch is another word for frequency. A musical note is a particular set of frequencies.

Have you ever sung "Row, Row, Row Your Boat"? To sing the notes, you make your larynx vibrate. The first three notes of the song are the same low pitch. The next two are higher.

The musical scale rises to higher pitches, too. It is divided into eight parts: Do, Re, Mi, Fa, So, La, Ti, Do. At "Do," your larynx vibrates slowest. Your larynx vibrates the most at "Ti."

They Made a Difference

Galileo Galilei

Galileo, an Italian astronomer and physicist, showed that frequency determines pitch. He scraped a chisel across a brass plate, causing screeches. Then he scraped the chisel at different speeds. He linked the pitch of the sounds to the spaces between the lines of shavings.

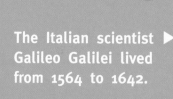

The Italian scientist ▶ Galileo Galilei lived from 1564 to 1642.

Experiment 3
Vibrations and Sound

- Place a ruler on the edge of a table.
- Make sure most of it sticks out from the edge.
- Firmly hold the end of the ruler on the tabletop.
- Now bang the other end of the ruler with your f[...]
- The ruler flips up and down, vibrating and makin[...] a sound.
- Now push the ruler in toward the table.
- What happens to the sound when less of the rul[...] sticks out?
- Move the ruler back out a little bit at a time an[...] it again to make it vibrate.
- Can you play "Row, Row, Row Your Boat" or the musical scale?
- What happens to the sound when you bang the ruler harder?

▲ The ruler can vibrate at certain pitches, or frequencies, depending on how much it sticks out.

The Doppler Effect

Have you ever stood on the platform of a train station and watched trains go by? When the engineer blows the whistle as a train passes, the sound changes. The pitch changes because the source of the sound is moving. The locomotive pushes the whistle's sound waves so they crowd together in front of it. That increases the waves' frequency. When the train leaves, the whistle's sound waves spread out again. They return to their usual frequency. Passengers hear the same pitch throughout because they are also moving.

This is the Doppler effect, named for Christian Johann Doppler. He observed it in 1842.

Everyday Science

To whisper, you take a small breath. When you shout, you take in more air. You exhale with greater force than you do for a whisper. The more energy a sound has, the louder it is.

◀ When the train approaches, its whistle has a higher pitch than normal.

Intensity and Loudness

Refraction due to different temperatures and high pitches can make sounds seem loud. But what really makes a sound intense is its energy. Refraction changes the direction of a wave. A sound's high pitch is due to its short wavelength.

What about the height of a wave? We call this measure of vibration **amplitude** (AM-pluh-tood). Amplitude controls a sound's intensity. The amplitude of a wave depends on the amount of energy a wave has. We measure amplitude in **decibels** (DEH-suh-bulz). A whisper is ten decibels. Thunder is 120 decibels. A jet plane taking off is 150 decibels.

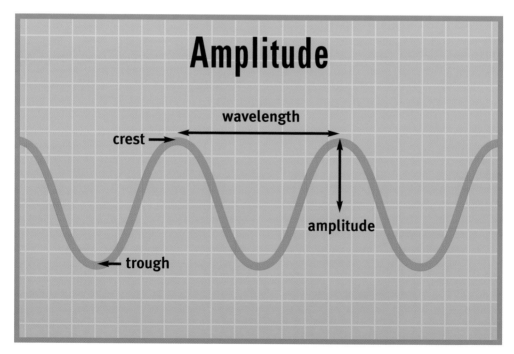

▲ Amplitude is how tall a wave is. The amplitude of a wave is measured from the midpoint to either the crest or the trough.

Chapter 3

Making Music

There are three types of musical instruments: string, percussion, and wind. Each instrument produces sound differently. To play a guitar or harp, you pluck or pick the strings. To play a violin or cello, you stroke the strings with a bow. Percussion instruments create sound when you strike them. Usually we think of drums, bells, cymbals, and xylophones as percussion instruments. A piano is a percussion instrument, too, because when you press down the keys, little hammers inside the piano hit its strings.

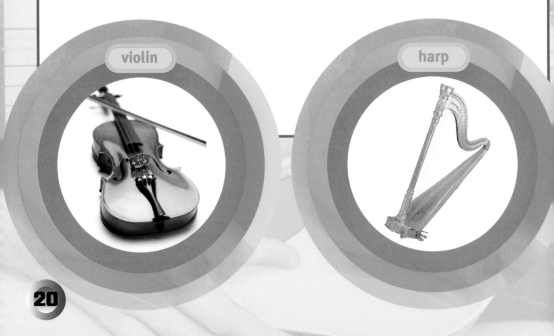

violin

harp

The pitch of a note depends on the length of the string. It also depends on how thick and tight the string is. A thin string that is tightly stretched gives off higher notes. Low-pitched notes come from thicker and looser strings.

When you play the guitar, you press six strings in order to shorten them. On the violin, you press four strings.

Drums are made of tightly stretched material. A drum vibrates when you strike it. A drum sounds high when the material is thin and stretched over a small circle. A lower sound comes from thicker material stretched over a bigger circle.

guitar

piano

▲ Fingers of the left hand hold down the strings, changing their pitch. The right hand strums the strings.

▲ A piano has strings inside, which get hit by small hammers. A piano is therefore a percussion instrument.

Experiment 4
Pulling Strings

- Get a cardboard shoebox.
- Get some rubber bands of different thicknesses.
- Stretch the rubber bands across the box.
- Pluck the rubber bands.
- Do the thick bands sound different from the thin ones? Can you describe the sound?
- Now push pencils underneath the rubber bands on each side of the shoebox.
- Pluck the rubber bands again.
- How do the rubber bands sound now? Are the strings the only things vibrating? You've just played a homemade guitar!
  - Press another pencil down on the rubber bands.
  - Slide the pencil back and forth while you pluck.
  - How do the pitches change? You've just played a homemade violin!

Experiment 5
Tooting Tubes

- Get eight bottles, all the same size, with narrow necks.
- Put them in a row.
- Fill each with water a little higher than the next.
- Put the bottom edge of your lower lip against the lip of one bottle.
- Now blow across the top.
- Do the same for all eight bottles.
- If you can't get a sound, tap each bottle with a spoon.
- Which bottle makes the highest sound? Which makes the lowest? Can you play "Do, Re, Mi, Fa, So, La, Ti, Do"? If not, try to tune the bottles by adding or pouring out water.

Wind instruments are usually wooden or metal tubes. The distance that the air travels through the tube determines the notes. To play the recorder and flute, you change the length of the tube by covering and uncovering holes. The farther the air travels, the lower the note.

Why do sounds from different instruments sound different? Why is a note made by strumming a string different from one made by blowing air? When a guitarist and a flutist both play the same note, you can tell which instrument created the note. These instruments are made of different materials and do not produce notes the same way. But that is not why the same note sounds different. No matter how they are produced, all notes vibrate at a main frequency.

They Made a Difference

In 1728, the Swiss mathematician Daniel Bernoulli showed that a string vibrates at a main frequency and contains harmonics. The main frequency is actually a blend of pitches. They can be divided into fractions.

In 1822, a French mathematician named Jean Baptiste Joseph Fourier described this idea with equations. They are now known as the Fourier series.

Electronic Music

Music can also be produced electronically by sound **synthesizers** (SIN-thuh-sigh-zerz). They make electronic signals that have the same frequencies as notes. Amplifiers send the notes to speakers or headphones that make the notes louder.

The first electronic synthesizer was the Moog. An engineer named Robert Moog invented it in the 1960s. The Moog changed the sound of music. It was very popular among jazz and rock musicians.

POINT

Picture It
Draw a picture of the musical instrument mentioned in Chapter 3 that you like best. Then write a caption describing the sound it makes.

▼ This Moog synthesizer was made in 1967.

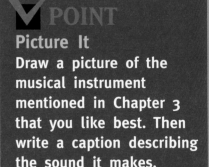

▲ Robert Moog

Careers

Acoustics is the study of sound. Acoustical engineers quiet noise in the environment. They create mufflers to soften the noise from car engines. They quiet sounds in buildings by using cork. They can also improve how well you hear a concert in an auditorium.

Chapter 4

Beyond Sound

In the late 1940s, pilots tried to fly planes faster than the speed of sound. Chuck Yeager and Joe Walker flew planes faster than sound in 1947. People said they "broke the sound barrier."

We call speeds faster than sound **supersonic** (soo-per-SAH-nik). When planes travel at supersonic speeds, they cause a loud crack, like thunder. This is called a sonic boom.

In the late 1960s, French and British airlines developed supersonic jets called the Concorde fleet. Concordes flew at twice the speed of sound.

Math Matters

The Concorde took about three hours to fly to Europe. Jets today take seven hours to fly that far. The Concorde fleet stopped flying in 2003.

Ultrasound

Many sounds have frequencies beyond human hearing. We call such sounds ultrasound. Ultrasound is similar to sonar that ships use.

Ultrasound can be used to clean jewelry. The ultra-high frequencies shake off dirt. Some dentists use ultrasound to clean teeth.

Ultrasound technology is also used to listen to the heartbeat of a baby while it is still inside its mother.

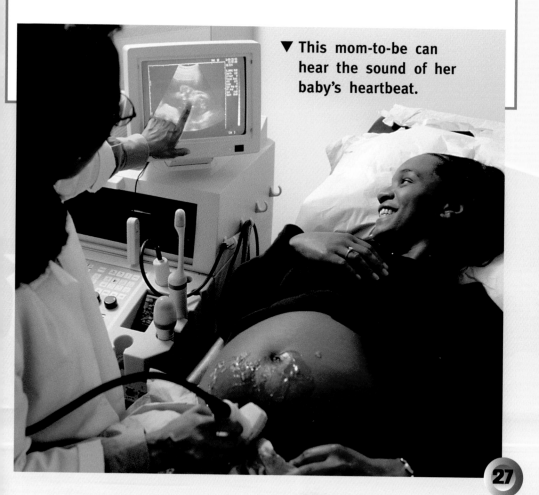

▼ This mom-to-be can hear the sound of her baby's heartbeat.

(((Conclusion)))

Sound is movement. Sound is caused by vibrations. The vibrations can travel through and around objects.

Sound is the basis for communication. Hearing sound is one of our five senses. We hear, see, smell, taste, and touch in order to survive.

accordion

Sound can give us joy when we use it to make music. It can annoy us when it is too loud. When sound is intense, it can help us communicate, or make it harder to communicate.

Using the energy of sound can help us avoid accidents. It can help us find food. It can also give us information so that we know if we are healthy. Sound can help us live longer and more joyful lives.

(((Sound)))

movement

vibration

energy

communication

Glossary

amplitude	(AM-pluh-tood) the height of a wave (page 19)
compress	(kum-PRES) push together, squeeze (page 5)
crest	(KREST) the highest part of a wave (page 15)
decibel	(DEH-suh-bul) a unit that measures the intensity of a sound (page 19)
diffraction	(dih-FRAK-shun) spreading out under an object as sound does after hitting an edge (page 13)
frequency	(FREE-kwen-see) the number of times a sound wave vibrates every second (page 15)
larynx	(LAIR-ingks) the part of the body that contains the vocal cords (page 5)
pitch	(PICH) the sound of a musical note, related to frequency (page 16)
rarefied	(RAIR-uh-fighd) having few particles to compress (page 5)
refract	(rih-FRAKT) to bend, as a light ray (page 11)
sonar	(SOH-nar) a sound system, usually used in water by ships, that uses echoes to find out how far away things are (page 10)
supersonic	(soo-per-SAH-nik) faster than the speed of sound (page 26)
synthesizer	(SIN-thuh-sigh-zer) an electronic device that makes musical notes (page 25)
trough	(TROFF) the lowest part of a wave (page 15)
vacuum	(VA-kyoom) the absence of air (page 8)
wavelength	(WAYV-lengkth) the distance between one crest and the next crest, or one trough and the next (page 15)

Index